D0908220

$18.05

THE
CHINCOTEAGUE
PONY

by Charlotte Wilcox

C A P S T O N E   P R E S S

M A N K A T O

LIBRARY #18,829 300657
DEXTER MUNICIPAL SCHOOLS
DEXTER, NEW MEXICO 8823

C A P S T O N E P R E S S

818 North Willow Street • Mankato, MN 56001

Copyright © 1996 Capstone Press. All rights reserved. No part of this book may be reproduced without written permission from the publisher.

Printed in the United States of America.

Library of Congress Cataloging-in Publication Data
Wilcox, Charlotte.
Chincoteague Ponies/by Charlotte Wilcox
p. cm.
Includes bibliographical references (p.45-46) and index.
Summary: Offers information about the breed of small horses which gets its
name from the island of Chincoteague located
off the coast of Maryland and Virginia
ISBN 1-56065-363-9
1. Chincoteague pony--Juvenile literature. [1. Chincoteague pony. 2. Ponies.
3 Horses.] I. Title.
SF315.2.C4W55 1996
636.1'6--dc20

95-47763
CIP
AC

Photo credits
Cheryl Blair: 6, 10, 19, 22, 26, 30, 36-37, 38, 40
Jean S. Buldain: 12, 14, 16, 20, 25, 28, 32, 34, 42

Table of Contents

Words in **boldface** type in the text are defined in the Glossary in the back of this book.

Quick Facts about
the Chincoteague Pony

Description

Height:	Chincoteagues are 12 to 13 1/2 **hands** from the ground to the top of the shoulders. That is 48 to 54 inches (122 to 137 centimeters) tall. Horses are measured in hands. One hand equals four inches (10 centimeters).
Weight:	Chincoteagues weigh 800 to 900 pounds (360 to 405 kilograms).
Physical features:	Chincoteague Ponies are actually small horses. They are very hardy, but some do not have a good build. This is improving with better breeding.
Colors:	They once were solid colors, but now many are spotted.

Development

History of breed:	Chincoteagues descended from European horses brought to Assateague Island by colonists in the 1600s. In the 20th century, **Welsh**, **Shetland**, and **pinto** bloodlines have been mixed with the Chincoteague.
Place of origin:	They originated on the islands of Chincoteague and Assateague off the coast of Maryland and Virginia.
Numbers:	About 150 adult ponies live on Assateague Island, with about 70 **foals** born each year. The foals are sold every summer.

Life History

Life span:	A well-cared-for Chincoteague Pony may live from 20 to 30 years.

Uses

The Chincoteague Ponies living on Assateague Island are wild. Most of the foals that are sold become children's riding ponies or pets.

Chapter 1

Famous Island Ponies

Some of the most famous ponies in the world live off the coast of the United States. They are the wild ponies of Assateague Island. The island is about five miles off the coast of Maryland and Virginia. The ponies are fenced in by the Atlantic Ocean. They share the island with birds, deer, and other wild animals.

The ponies are called Chincoteague Ponies. They are named for the nearby smaller island of Chincoteague. People have cared for them for hundreds of years. Only a few hundred ponies have ever lived on Assateague Island at one time.

Original Chincoteague Ponies were solid shades. Today they can be spotted.

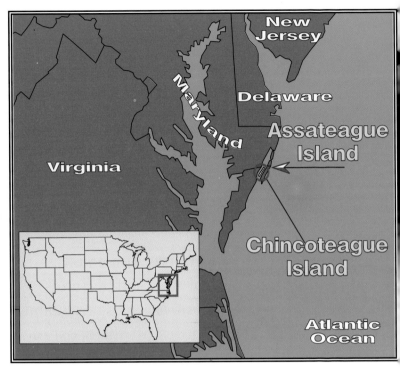

The northern part of Assateague Island is in Maryland, and the southern part is in Virginia. Most of the ponies live in Virginia.

The Annual Pony Swim

About 70 ponies are born on Assateague Island every year. If they all stayed on the island, there would be so many ponies that they would not have enough food. For about 300 years, the people of Chincoteague Island have made sure that does not happen.

People from Chincoteague round up the ponies once every summer. The ponies take a short swim across the bay to Chincoteague Island. They swim about one-quarter to one-half mile (.4 to .8 kilometers). They are herded by people in boats.

Thousands of people come to watch this special roundup. It is the oldest roundup in North America. People buy the foals that are old enough to be separated from their mothers. The rest of the ponies swim back to Assateague Island for another year.

A Famous Book

Almost 50 years ago, a famous children's book told the story of the ponies and people of Chincoteague. The book was called *Misty of Chincoteague*. It was written by Marguerite Henry. She later wrote three more books about Chincoteague Ponies. Many children came to know and love Chincoteague Ponies through her books.

Chapter 2
How They Got There

Many stories are told about the ponies of Assateague Island. One story says that they were in a shipwreck and swam to the island during a storm. Another story says they were left behind by colonists who gave up farming and moved away.

The stories are partly true and partly false. The Chincoteague Ponies are descended from horses that came on ships from Europe. They probably arrived safely instead of being shipwrecked. They were owned by colonists, but they were not deserted.

Horses in a New Land

There were no horses on the continent when Europeans came to North America around

Chincoteagues swim between islands.

1500. The first horses in North America arrived with Spanish explorers. More horses, cattle, sheep, and pigs came later from England and France.

There were no fields of grain or hay to feed the animals. People kept them in **pastures** where they could eat grass. There were no fences to keep the animals from running off. People had to find other ways to hold the animals.

Grassy islands made good pastures. Most animals can swim without being taught, but horses usually will not cross water unless they are forced. Small islands close to the eastern shore of North America became home to horses, cattle, sheep, and pigs during the 1600s and 1700s. The water was a natural fence.

Farmers from each town let their animals run together on the islands. They branded the animals with a mark to show who owned them. People took turns guarding the animals from wolves and wildcats.

Chincoteague Ponies run wild on Assateague Island.

North America's First Roundups

The animals stayed on the islands until they were needed. Then everyone got together to round them up. Pens were built to sort them out. Each new foal, calf, lamb, or piglet was branded with the mark of its mother. Sheep were sheared, cattle and pigs were butchered, and horses were caught to use in the fields.

People called these roundups "penning." The penning days became big celebrations with food, music, and games. One of the most popular events was watching people try to handle the young horses that came off the islands. The younger horses were not used to being around humans. They put up quite a fight when their training began.

As time went by, farmers on the mainland built barns and fences to keep their animals closer to home. People quit using island pastures. Penning days became a thing of the past in many places, but not on Chincoteague and Assateague islands.

Chincoteague Ponies eat 12 pounds (4.5 kilograms) of grass or hay a day.

Chapter 3

Pony Penning

During the 1800s, horses were in great demand. Several horse farmers kept large herds of horses on Chincoteague, Assateague, and nearby islands.

By the late 1800s, people were coming from Washington, D.C., Philadelphia, and New York to watch the pony penning. Hotels on Chincoteague overflowed with visitors. Horses on nearby islands were rounded up. They were taken in boats to Chincoteague for the penning.

Assateague Becomes an Animal Refuge

By the 1890s, Chincoteague Island had a good-size town. It had a post office,

Chincoteagues are still raised on Assateague Island.

businesses, and houses. Farmers had to build fences to keep their animals out of town. Assateague Island was different. It had only a small village with a few fishermen's houses and a lighthouse.

In 1917, a man from Baltimore bought much of the land in the southern half of Assateague. He would not let the fishermen cross his property to get from their houses to the bay where they fished.

Assateague fishermen soon moved their homes onto Chincoteague. They were tired of making the long, roundabout trip to the cove every day. The village of Assateague was gone by the early 1920s. Assateague Island once again belonged to the ponies and other farm animals, along with wildlife and birds.

Disasters

Things were changing. People no longer needed to travel by horse and buggy. They were driving cars instead.

Chincoteagues have short, sturdy bodies with long tails.

About 70 ponies are born on Assateague Island each year.

Farmers still raised horses on the islands, but fewer and fewer people wanted to buy them.

Then, two disasters hit the town of Chincoteague. In 1920, a huge fire roared through the town. It destroyed many houses and businesses. People rebuilt them, but four years later the same thing happened.

The fires were the worst things ever to happen on the island. But they turned out to be a good thing for the ponies.

In 1924, people on the island started the Chincoteague Volunteer Fire Company. They decided to meet together and train to fight fires. But they knew they would have to get better gear to make sure another fire did not destroy the town.

The next year, the firefighters decided to hold a carnival on pony-penning days. They wanted to raise money for firefighting equipment. They also decided to swim the ponies from Assateague to Chincoteague instead of putting them on boats.

The Pony Swim Begins

The 1925 pony penning and firefighters' carnival were huge successes. About 15,000 people crowded onto the little island of Chincoteague to watch the pony swim. There were pony races, swimming races, and boat races.

Farmers donated 15 or 20 foals. The firefighters sold the males for $75 and the females for $90. They raised enough money that year to buy a new firetruck.

The ponies enjoy a happy life on Assateague Island.

The pony swim turned Chincoteague's little festival into a big, exciting event. In 1935, a film crew came to Chincoteague to film the pony swim. Soon people from all over the country wanted to see this unique roundup.

A Refuge for Wildlife

Chincoteague's pony swim became an important money-raising event for the town and its firefighters. The ponies enjoyed a happy life on Assateague. They swam to Chincoteague once a year to delight the crowds. Then they returned to their island home. But fewer farmers kept horses on the islands.

In 1943, the U.S. government decided to protect the animals and birds on the islands. The government established the Chincoteague National Wildlife Refuge. The refuge is not on Chincoteague at all. It is on the south end of Assateague. It is 13 miles long. The rest of Assateague Island later became a park.

The Fire Company Takes Another Step

Also in the 1940s, the Chincoteague Volunteer Fire Company decided to help preserve the Chincoteague Pony. With fewer horse farmers keeping island herds, the firefighters decided to buy their own horses. They wanted to keep the pony swim going. They asked for permission to keep their ponies in the new wildlife refuge on Assateague.

The fire company bought ponies from one of the last horse farmers on the island. These ponies were still much like the mixed-breed horses used by early pioneers. They were small, mostly dark colored, and very hardy. But the ponies suffered from inbreeding. This happens when animals that are too closely related breed with each other.

Inbreeding caused some of the island ponies to have weak bones and joints. They were not as pretty as other breeds. The firefighters set out to do something about this problem. They brought in Welsh and pinto horses to breed with the Chincoteague Ponies. They also brought in **mustangs** from the western United States. But the mustangs could not get used to the island climate. Many of them died.

The firefighters of Chincoteague were just as good at horse breeding as they were at roundups and carnivals. Soon they had more than 100 healthy horses on the island. They turned their original herd into a breed of beautiful, talented ponies with its own **registry.**

No more than 150 adult ponies can live on the island at one time. The rest are sold at the pony sale.

Chapter 4

The Story of Misty

In 1946, Marguerite Henry came to Chincoteague. Henry was a famous children's author. She wanted to watch the pony swim.

Her book, *Misty of Chincoteague*, came out the next year. In the book, Henry told the story of the ponies and people of Chincoteague. The characters in *Misty of Chincoteague* were real people and real horses that Henry met when she visited the island.

Misty was a young foal when she swam with her mother to the 1946 pony penning. Henry fell in love with Misty. So did a young brother and sister from Chincoteague. They were Paul and Maureen Beebe. Their grandfather, Clarence Beebe, was one of the

Marguerite Henry wrote many stories about Chincoteague Ponies.

old-time horse farmers on the islands. Misty went to live at the Beebe farm.

Weathering the Storm

In the spring of 1962, a storm swept over the islands of Chincoteague and Assateague. Almost half of the people living on Chincoteague had to leave their homes. The storm killed thousands of birds and animals. It killed some of the young foals on Assateague.

At the Beebe farm, the family brought Misty into the house to ride out the storm. Right there in the kitchen, Misty gave birth to her most famous filly. She was named Stormy.

When the storm was over, the Chincoteague firefighters set to work caring for the horses that survived. The Beebe family took Misty on tour to help raise money to rebuild the herd.

The next year, Henry told the exciting story of Stormy's birth in her book *Stormy, Misty's Foal*. Stormy introduced a new generation of readers to the Chincoteague Pony, almost 20 years after Henry first wrote about Misty.

Chincoteague's Pony Penning Days are always held the last Wednesday and Thursday of July.

Most foals that are sold become children's riding ponies.

Misty and the Beebe Family

Misty lived all her life on the island. She died in 1972 at the age of 26. Maureen Beebe still lives on Chincoteague. The Beebe farm where Maureen and Misty grew up is still there, too.

Misty had several foals. The last one, Stormy, died in 1993. Some of Misty's grandchildren are still living.

Though some of them live far away now, a few of Misty's relatives are brought back to Chincoteague in July to join the celebration. With their glossy coats, bright eyes, and flowing **manes** and tails, they look quite different from the shaggy island ponies that come ashore at pony penning.

Misty Today

The story of Misty is still alive. In 1961, a film company turned the story of Misty into a movie called *Misty*. It is now available on video.

Henry also wrote more Chincoteague books. The books were very popular. They are still available in bookstores and at the library.

Many people visit or write the Beebe Gallery. It is run by Maureen Beebe on Chincoteague Island. The gallery has pictures and other special things from Misty's life.

Chapter 5
The Ponies Today

Only horses born on Assateague, Chincoteague, and nearby islands, or those who are descended from a horse that was born on the islands can be called Chincoteague Ponies. In 1994, the Chincoteague Volunteer Fire Company established the Chincoteague Pony Association. It keeps a registry of these ponies.

The registry keeps track of ponies and their **pedigrees**. People who own a Chincoteague Pony and raise a foal of their own can register the pony. Ponies purchased at the pony penning sale are also registered. If the pony was not born on Assateague Island, the owner must be

Island ponies look shaggy because they are outside in all kinds of weather.

LIBRARY #18,829
DEXTER MUNICIPAL SCHOOLS
DEXTER, NEW MEXICO 88

able to prove that both the pony's parents were Chincoteague Ponies.

What a Chincoteague Pony Looks Like

Today's Chincoteague Ponies look different from the early ponies. They are about the same size but are prettier and more colorful. When trained, they get along well with people. They make good riding ponies and pets.

Horses are measured in hands. A hand is four inches (10 centimeters). A horse's height is measured from the **withers** to the ground. Most Chincoteague Ponies stand between 12 and 13 1/2 hands.

An adult Chincoteague Pony weighs between 800 and 900 pounds (360 and 405 kilograms). They have short, sturdy bodies with long manes and tails. Chincoteague Ponies have strong hooves. They can gallop very fast for horses their size.

The original Chincoteague Ponies were all solid shades of reddish-brown, brown, and black. But when Welsh, Shetland, and pinto **stallions** were brought to the islands, they

Chincoteagues come in many colors.

Flank

Loins

Hindquarters

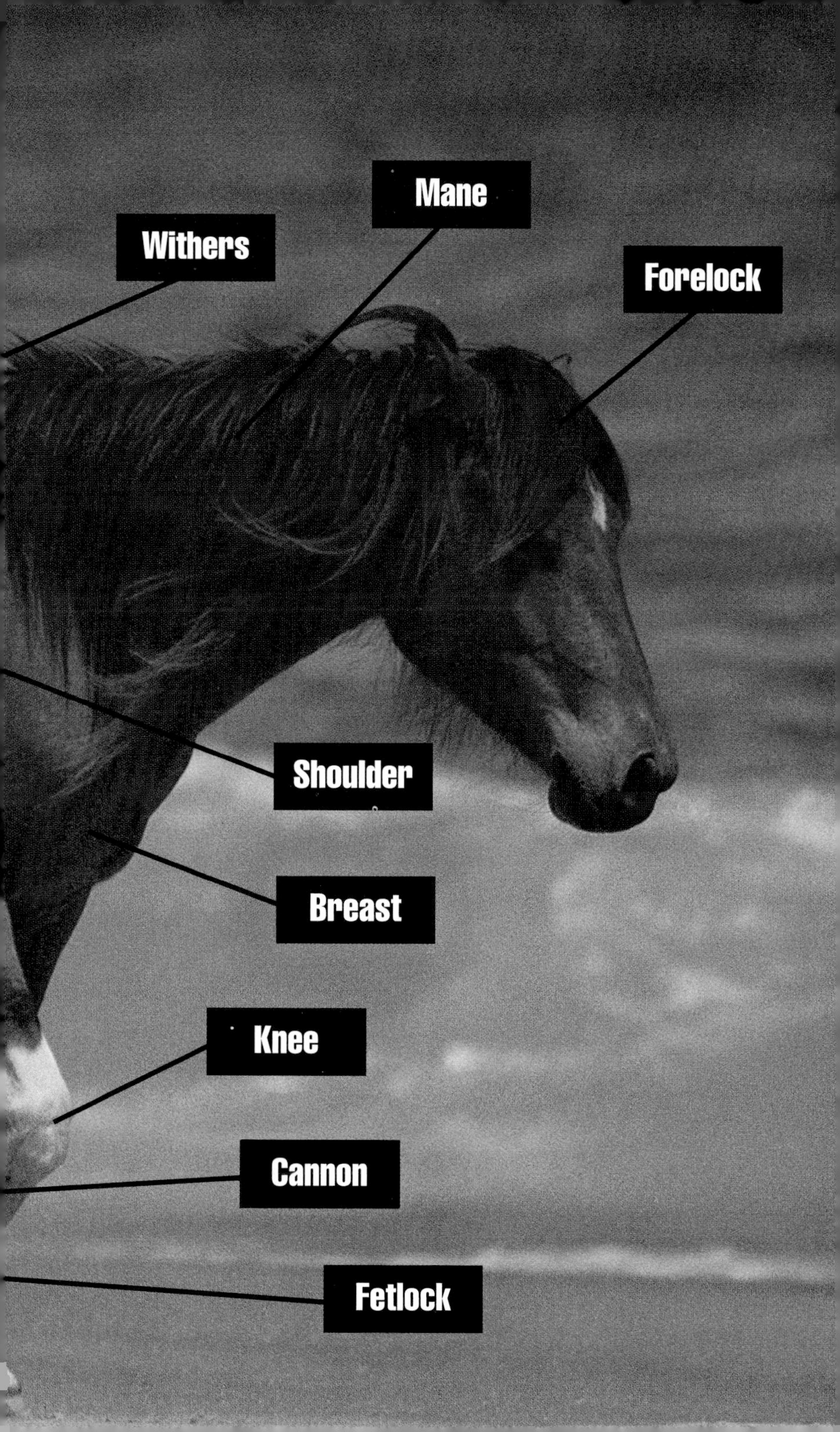

Withers

Mane

Forelock

Shoulder

Breast

Knee

Cannon

Fetlock

passed on brighter coloring. Today Chincoteague Ponies come in all colors. They can be spotted, **palomino**, gray, white, or **buckskin**, as well as darker in color.

Breeding of Chincoteague Ponies

The ponies that stay on Assateague Island live in a protected wildlife area. The government has decided that no more than 150 adult ponies can live on the island at one time. About 15 or 20 ponies are stallions. The rest are **mares.**

Each stallion keeps from five to 15 mares in his own group. The stallion breeds with the mares in his group. The ponies breed most often in the spring. Each year, about half of the mares get pregnant. The foals are born 11 months later.

Foals live mostly on milk for their first few weeks. They stay close to their mothers so they can drink whenever they want. But soon they want to play with the other foals. They start nibbling on grass. They become more independent.

Once Chincoteagues are tamed, they love people.

Chapter 6
A Visit to the Islands

Assateague Island is divided between the states of Maryland and Virginia. The northern part of the island is in Maryland and the southern part is in Virginia. Most of the ponies live in the Chincoteague National Wildlife Refuge in Virginia. The rest of the island is Maryland's Assateague State Park and Assateague Island National Seashore, a national park.

A separate herd of wild ponies lives on the Maryland end of the island. They are not owned by the Chincoteague firefighters and are not rounded up for pony penning.

Pony Penning Days

Chincoteague's Pony Penning Days are always held the last Wednesday and Thursday

Most of the ponies live at the Chincoteague National Wildlife Refuge.

A well-cared-for Chincoteague may live for 30 years.

of July. The roundup on Assateague begins on Wednesday morning. The firefighters must schedule the swim at a time when the ponies can cross the channel at low tide. Sometimes they do not know the exact time until the day before.

The swim from Assateague to Chincoteague does not take very long. About 200 horses and foals make the swim. When the ponies come onto the beach on Chincoteague, they are given time to rest. Then the firefighters herd them through town to the pens on the other side of the island. Thousands of visitors line the streets to get a look.

The Pony Auction

Thursday is the day people can buy the ponies. The average price is about $1,000. Over the last 50 years, Chincoteague Ponies have been sold to people from every part of the United States and Canada. Some have gone as far as England.

Some people who buy a Chincoteague Pony do not want to bring it home. They want the pony to stay wild and free on Assateague Island. Each year, the fire company allows 10 people to buy a female pony to send back to the island. This system keeps the herd going by replacing the old mares that have died.

A Special Horse

The ponies on Assateague are not used to being around people. Most will run away from a person. Some may bite or kick. Park rangers on Assateague warn visitors not to pet or feed the Chincoteague Ponies.

But once they are tamed, the Chincoteagues learn to love people. They are kind and beautiful horses with a colorful history.

Glossary

buckskin—a tan horse with black legs, mane, and tail

foal—a young horse

hand—a unit of measurement equal to four inches (10 centimeters)

mane—the long hair growing on the top of a horse's head and down the neck

mare—a female horse

mustang—wild horses of the western United States

palomino—a golden horse with a silvery-white mane and tail

pasture—an open field, usually fenced, where animals eat grass

pedigree—a list of a horse's ancestors

pinto—a horse marked with patches of white and another color

registry—an organization that keeps track of official pedigrees for a particular horse breed

Shetland—a small, muscular pony breed from the Shetland Islands off Scotland
stallion—a male horse
Welsh—a pony breed from Wales, known for its elegant beauty
withers—the top of a horse's shoulders

To Learn More

Edwards, Elwyn Hartley. *Encyclopedia of the Horse.* New York: Dorling Kindersley, 1994.

Harris, Susan. *The United States Pony Club Manual of Horsemanship: Basics for Beginners.* New York: Howell Book House, 1994.

Henry, Marguerite. *Misty of Chincoteague.* Chicago: Rand McNally & Company, 1947.

Richter, Judy. *Pony Talk: A Complete Learning Guide for Young Riders.* New York: Howell Book House, 1993.

You can read articles about Chincoteague Ponies in the following magazines: *Discover Horses, Equus, Horse and Horseman, Horse and Pony, Just About Horses,* and *Young Rider.*

Useful Addresses

American Youth Horse Council
4193 Iron Works Pike
Lexington, KY 40511-2742

Assateague State Park
Route 611
7307 Stephen Decatur Highway
Berlin, MD 21811

Beebe Gallery
209D Maddox Boulevard
Chincoteague Island, VA 23336

Canadian Horse Council
P.O. Box 156
Rexdale, ON M9W 5L2
Canada

Chincoteague Chamber of Commerce
P.O. Box 258
Chincoteague, VA 23336

Chincoteague National Wildlife Refuge
P.O. Box 62
Chincoteague, VA 23336

Chincoteague Pony Association
P.O. Box 691
Chincoteague Island, VA 23336

Misty of Chincoteague Foundation
P.O. Box 4352
Charlottesville, VA 29905

Index